Adrian Mitchell was born in London in 1932. An ex-reporter, he is widely acclaimed as a poet, lyricist, novelist and writer for television and the stage. He has adapted plays for, among other people, the Royal Shakespeare and National Theatre Companies as well as instigating and script-editing many shows written by groups of adults and children. He was one of the originators of the public poetry movement and now performs his poems extensively in Britain, Europe and the United States. He has won an Eric Gregory Award and was during 1980-81 Judith E. Wilson Fellow at Cambridge.

Adrian Mitchell's books include the poetry collections OUT LOUD, RIDE THE NIGHTMARE, THE APEMAN COMETH and FOR BEAUTY DOUGLAS (Collected Poems 1953-79) and the novels IF YOU SEE ME COMIN', THE BODYGUARD and WARTIME. His first collection of poems for children, NOTHINGMAS DAY, is published in 1984.

ON THE BEACH AT CAMBRIDGE
New Poems

by
ADRIAN MITCHELL

Allison & Busby
London   .   New York

First published in Great Britain in 1984 by
Allison & Busby Ltd
6a Noel Street
London W1V 3RB
and distributed in the USA by
Schocken Books Inc
200 Madison Avenue
New York, NY 10016

British Library Cataloguing in Publication Data
Mitchell, Adrian
    On the beach at Cambridge.
    I. Title
    821'.914   PR6063.177

    ISBN 0–85031–563–8
    ISBN 0–85031–564–6 Pbk

Set in 11/12 Univers by
Falcon Graphic Art Ltd, Wallington, Surrey
Printed and bound in Great Britain by
Richard Clay (The Chaucer Press) Ltd, Bungay, Suffolk

Acknowledgements

Most of these poems have not been published before, but all of them have been used in my performances of poetry. My special thanks to those who organized those performances and those who came to them.

Dedication

This book is dedicated to the true socialists and anarchists of the world.

Educational Health Warning

None of the work in this or any of my other books is to be used in connection with any examination whatsoever. (But I'm happy if they're read aloud in schools by people who like them enough to read them aloud.)

Contents

ON THE BEACH AT CAMBRIDGE

What Is Poetry?

(for Sasha, Daniella, Vladko and Martin Shurbanov)

Look at those naked words dancing together!
Everyone's very embarrassed.
Only one thing to do about it —
Off with your clothes
And join in the dance.
Naked words and people dancing together.
There's going to be trouble.
Here come the Poetry Police!

Keep dancing.

Back In The Playground Blues

I dreamed I was back in the playground, I was about four
feet high
Yes dreamed I was back in the playground, standing about
four feet high
Well the playground was three miles long and the
playground was five miles wide

It was broken black tarmac with a high wire fence all
around
Broken black dusty tarmac with a high fence running all
around
And it had a special name to it, they called it The Killing
Ground

Got a mother and a father, they're one thousand years
away
The rulers of The Killing Ground are coming out to play
Everybody thinking: "Who they going to play with today?"

Well you get it for being Jewish
And you get it for being black
Get it for being chicken
And you get it for fighting back
You get it for being big and fat
Get it for being small
Oh those who get it get it and get it
For any damn thing at all

Sometimes they take a beetle, tear off its six legs one by
    one
Beetle on its black back, rocking in the lunchtime sun
But a beetle can't beg for mercy, a beetle's not half the
    fun

I heard a deep voice talking, it had that iceberg sound
"It prepares them for Life" — but I have never found
Any place in my life worse than The Killing Ground.

To A Critic

You don't go to Shakespeare for statistics
You don't go to bed for a religious service
But you want poems like metal mental mazes —
Excuse me while I nervous.

A song can carry so many facts
A song can lift plenty of story
A song can score jokes and curses too
And any amount of glory

But if you overload your dingadong song
With theoretical baggage
Its wings tear along the dotted line
And it droppeth to earth like a cabbage

Yes it droppeth to earth like a bloody great cabbage
And the cabbage begins to rot.
My songs may be childish as paper planes
But they glide — so thanks a lot.

Lament For The Welsh Makers

WILLIAM DUNBAR sang piteously
When he mourned for the Makers of poetry.
He engraved their names with this commentary —
Timor mortis conturbat me.

DUNBAR, I'm Scot-begotten too,
But I would celebrate a few
Welsh masters of the wizardry —
The fear of death moves inside me.

"After the feasting, silence fell."
ANEIRIN knew how the dead smell.
Now he has joined their company.
The fear of death moves inside me.

TALIESIN, born of earth and clay,
Primroses, the ninth wave's spray
And nettle flowers, where is he?
The fear of death moves inside me.

LLYWARCH's sons numbered twenty-four.
Each one was eaten by the war.
He lived to curse senility.
The fear of death moves inside me.

TALHAEARN and AROFAN,
AFAN FERDDIG and MORFRAN
Are lost, with all their poetry.
The fear of death moves inside me.

MYRDDIN sang, a silver bell,
But from the battlefield he fell
Into a deep insanity.
The fear of death moves inside me.

GWALCHMAI, who sang of Anglesey
And a girl like snowfall on a tree
And lions too, lies silently —
The fear of death moves inside me.

CYNDDELW's balladry was sold
For women's kisses and men's gold.
His shop is shut permanently.
The fear of death moves inside me.

HYWEL chanted Meirionnydd's charm.
His pillow was a girl's white arm.
Now he is whiter far than she.
The fear of death moves inside me.

PRYDYDD y MOCH would smile to see
An Englishman — if he was maggoty.
Now he is grinning bonily.
The fear of death moves inside me.

DAFYDD ap GWILYM did women much good
At the cuckoo's church in the green wood.
Death ended his sweet ministry.
The fear of death moves inside me.

GWERFYL MECHAIN wrote in cheerful tones
Of the human body's tropical zones.
She shared DAFYDD's hot philosophy.
The fear of death moves inside me.

IOLO GOCH wrote of any old thing —
Girls, feasts and even an English King.
They say he died most professionally.
The fear of death moves inside me.

GRUFFUDD GRYG wept desperately
For the North of Wales in her poverty.
He was a bird from heaven's country.
The fear of death moves inside me.

LLYWELYN GOGH's fist dared to knock
On the heavy door with the black steel lock.
A skull told him its history.
The fear of death moves inside me.

SION CENT, who sang thank you to his purse,
RHYS GOGH, who killed a fox with verse,
Sleep in the gravel dormitory.
The fear of death moves inside me.

IEUAN ap RHYDDERCH so scholarly,
GWERFUL MADOG of famed hospitality,
LEWYS GLYN COTHI who loved luxury —
The fear of death moves inside me.

DAFYDD ap EDMWND'S singing skill
Thrilled through all Wales. Then it fell still.
LEWYS MON wrote his elegy.
The fear of death moves inside me.

BEDO BRWNLLYS, IEUAN DEULWYN,
GUTYN OWAIN, TUDUR PENLLYN,
All exiles in Death's monarchy.
The fear of death moves inside me.

Life was dark-coloured to TUDUR ALED.
WILLIAM LLYN brooded on the dead.
SION TUDUR mocked all vanity.
The fear of death moves inside me.

DIC HUWS dedicated a roundelay
To a girl by the name of Break of Day.
Night broke on both of them, remorselessly —
The fear of death moves inside me.

And hundreds have since joined the towering choir —
Poets of Wales, like trees on fire,
Light the black twentieth century.
The fear of death moves inside me.

Oh DYLAN THOMAS, as bright as nails,
Could make no kind of a living in Wales
So he died of American charity.
The fear of death moves inside me.

Terror of death, terror of death,
Terror of death, terror of death,
That drumbeat sounds relentlessly.
The fear of death moves inside me.

Since we must all of us ride down
The black hill into the black town,
Let us sing out courageously.
The fear of death moves inside me.

The black lungs swell, the black harp sighs,
Whenever a Welsh maker dies.
Forgive my nervous balladry.
Timor mortis conturbat me.

The Owl Song

(After watching a terrible battle, Merlin decides to live as
an owl in a wood.)

I have walked through the valley of slate
And the rain was blue
I have seen the sky like a hunter's net
Deepest darkest blue
I have seen the bit tight in the horse's teeth
And the bit was blue
I have heard swords sing on the battlefield
And the swords were blue
I have seen the eyes of my dead foe
They were round as the world and blue
I have seen the face of my friend in the dawn
On the sheep-shorn grass — his face was blue

      Blue grave
     Blue gravel on a grave
Blue flowers on the gravel on a grave

And I shall wake in the blue night
And sleep in the blue day
And I will live my own blue life
In the blue tree   In the blue tree

And my food shall be blue
And my wine shall be blue
And my mind shall be filled
With nothing but blue

blue   blue   blue   blue   blue   blue

Farm Animals

Clotted cream sheep
We troop in a dream
Through the steep deep wool
Of a yellow meadow
We are oblong and boring
We are all alike
Liking to be all alike

And the grass-like grass
Is alike, all alike, and all we think
Is grass grass grass
Yes grass is all we think
And all we do
Is wool

But that's the deal, the ancient deal,
The wonderful deal between sheep and men

Men give grass
We come across with wool

That agreement was signed
On the green baize table in Eden

What would happen if we broke the contract?
Oh that would be mutiny, we would be punished
By being eaten, we would deserve to be eaten.
But of course we never rebel, so we are never eaten.

On The Verses Entitled "Farm Animals"

The stereotypical tra-a-avesty opposite
Purports to speak for sheep
Nothing could be more cra-a-assly human

Despite our similar coiffures
Each sheep's a separate planet
With its own opinions and visions

All that we share is the furnace heart
Of all long-distance serfs
We're hot and getting hotter
So shepherds, you better watch your flocks

A. Ram.

December Cat

Among the scribbled tangle
of the branches of that garden tree
only about two hundred
lime-coloured leaves still shudder

but the hunting cat
perched in the middle of the scribble
believes he's invisible
to the few sparrows visiting
the tips of the tree

like a giant soldier
standing in a grey street at noon
wearing a bright ginger uniform
hung with guns
hung with grenades
who holds a sprig of heather up
as he shouts to the houses:
Come out! It's all right,
I'm only a hillside!

The Airline Steward's Spiel

Oxygen masks
Four at each side
Whenever you see one
You need one
So grab one

I've never
Seen them come down
And my wife and I
Would like to keep it that way

Have a pleasant flight

Commuting The Wrong Way Round Early Morning

Caught the Gospel Oak train
At the dog-end of Tuesday night.
Camden Town darkness
Laying like gravy on a plate . . .
But at Liverpool Street Station
They've got a smudgey brand of blue daylight.

Here comes half the Essex population
Tensed up for their desky work.
I'm struggling up a waterfall —
Bubbling secretaries, rocky clerks.
For I'm off to Billericay
Like a sausage on a fork.

The Call

(or Does The Apple Tree Hate Plums?)

i was standing in my room
the whirling tape was singing:
i'm never going back
i'm never going back.

i read four lines by Elaine Feinstein
the tears jumped in my eyes.
i read eight lines by Allen Ginsberg
and electricity sprang
from the soles of my feet
and the electric flames
danced on the roof of my skull.

someone calling
my self calling to myself
the call i'd been hoping for

let yourself sing it said
let yourself dance
let yourself be
an apple tree

i wrote this daftness down
then smiled and smiled
and said aloud
thank you thank you

you may want money
you may want pears
you may want bayonets
or tears

shake me as hard as you like
only apples will fall

apples   apples   and apples

For My Son

"The next best thing to the human tear" . . . advertising
slogan for an eyewash.

The next best thing to the human tear
Is the human smile
Which beams at us reflected white
For a lunar while.
But smiles congeal. Two eyes alight
With water cannot glow for long,
And a better thing than the human tear
Is the human song.

If cigarette or city burn
The smoke breaks into air.
So your breath, cries and laughter turn
And are abandoned there.
Once I had everything to learn
And thought each book had pretty pages.
Now I don't even trust the sun
Which melts like butter through the ages.

Nevertheless, crack-voiced I'll sing
For you, who drink the generous light
Till, fat as happiness, you sing
Your gay, immortal appetite.
I bring you air, food, grass and rain,
Show you the breast where you belong.
You take them all and sing again
Your human song.

The Swan

The anger of the swan
Burns black
Over ambitious eyes.

The power of the swan
Flexes steel wings
To batter feeble air.

The beauty of the swan
Is the sermon
Preached between battles.

One More Customer Satisfied

He staggered through the cities moaning for melons:
"Green melons streaked with yellow!
Yellow melons tinged with green!
Don't try to fool me. They fooled me before
With tie-dyed green-and-yellow footballs
And the breasts of yellow women, green-tinted
  nipples. . . ."

In his yellow rage and his green longing
He rolled himself into a melon-shaped heap of
  hopelessness
Crying out: "Melons! Bring out your melons!"

So they took a million melons to Cape Kennedy,
Scooped them out, filled them with green and yellow
  paint
And splattered them all over the bright side of the
  moon.

They adjusted his face so it faced the face of the moon
And they told him: "There is your one true melon,
Your forever melon, your melon of melons."

Now, fully grateful, he watches the melon rise,
The setting of the melon, the new melon and the full
  melon,
With a smile like a slice of melon in the green-and-
  yellow melon-light.

lo, lo, It's Off To Work We Go

To be seduced by a cloud
It's like wrestling with a weightless bear
He was all around me in and out of me
Whispering his small rain everywhere

Now I am an old walking woman
My skin is like yellow leather
But I keep half an eye cocked at the sky
And I smile when they talk about the weather

So when the sky gets randy to rain
I never run for cover
For a man is only a fool on a stick
But a cloud is a total lover

Brazil Nut In Edinburgh

Strapping upon her head the brand-new sporran
Dolores hoped she did not look too foreign

For Julietta, Who Asked For An Epitaph

The half-dead shone with double life
When magicked by her liveliness.
Over the woods she used to go
Flying in her flying dress.

But Death was depressed.
He took Julietta.
She smiled and danced with him.
Now Death feels better.

A Wise Woman

Woman called Sarah born with nothing but looks and
    lust
I saw her on her deathbed she was smiling fit to bust
She said: I've lived my life on the Golden Triangle
    plan —
Don't play with razors, don't pay your bills, don't
    boogie with a married man.

Happy Fiftieth Deathbed

D H Lawrence on the dodgem cars
Sniffing the smell of the electric stars
Cool black angel jumps up beside
Sorry David Herbert it's the end of your ride

Thank you very much Mr D H Lawrence
Thank you very much
Thank you very much Mr D H Lawrence
For The Rainbow and such

D H Lawrence with naughty Mrs Brown
Trying to play her hurdy-gurdy upside-down
In comes Mr Brown and he says Veronica
May I accompany on my harmonica

Thank you very much Mr D H Lawrence
Thank you very much
Thank you very much Mr D H Lawrence
Back to your hutch

D H Lawrence met Freud in a dream
Selling stop me and buy one Eldorado ice cream
Siggie says you ought to call your stories
Knickerbocker Splits and Banana Glories

Thank you very much Mr D H Lawrence
Thank you very much
Thank you very much Mr D H Lawrence
Keep in touch

September Love Poem

I flop into our bed with Thee,
Ovaltine and warm milk-o
And there we lie in ecstasy
Watching Sergeant Bilko.

Astrid-Anna

(This piece was written especially for an Anglo-German audience at the Goethe Institute in London)

Here is a news item from a right-wing British paper — the *Daily Mail*.

"TERROR GIRL IS ILL"
"Baader Meinhof girl Astrid Proll, who faces extradition to Germany, is physically and mentally ill, her friends said yesterday. They gathered outside Bow Street magistrates court . . . and handed out leaflets saying she was having difficulty in breathing and had 'sensations of panic'. Carnations were thrown to her as she was led away."

If Astrid Proll, who is now a British citizen by marriage — Anna Puttick — is sent back to Germany, she will be dead within two years. There are special sections in special prisons in Germany where prisoners like Astrid-Anna find it easy to obtain revolvers. Even odder, they do not shoot their jailers. They shoot out their own brains. If the British hand over Astrid-Anna to the West German police, we will be collaborating in yet another murder. Well, we done a few before.

> Sensations of panic
> Carnations were thrown
> Free Astrid   Free Anna

Astrid-Anna was accused of the attempted murder of two policemen.
But she has never been found guilty of anything.
But she was the first prisoner in Germany to be kept in conditions of SENSORY DEPRIVATION. In the Silent Wing of the

Women's Psychiatric Unit at Ossendorf Prison in Cologne.

There are white walls, constant lighting, no external sounds — techniques designed to disorientate and subdue. She spent a total of FOUR AND A HALF MONTHS in the Silent Wing. About TWENTY-FOUR WEEKS in the Silent Wing. About ONE THOUSAND SEVEN HUNDRED HOURS in the Silent Wing.

Her trial was stopped by a doctor. He found the following complaints: weakness and exhaustion, the feeling of "being wrapped in cotton wool", dizziness, blackouts, headaches and no appetite, feelings of breaking down, an inability to concentrate, increasing signs of phobia and agoraphobia. Her blood circulation began to collapse, depriving her brain of oxygen. Continued imprisonment, said the doctor, would lead to PERMANENT AND IRREPARABLE DAMAGE.

Four and a half months
In the silent wing
Four and a half months
in the silent wing

Shut in a white box
Under the constant neon
Being whitened in a box
Under the silent neon
Boxed in the white neon
Of the silent box
Under the constant wing.

Silenced in the white
Under the white wing
Of the constant box of neon

In the white of the silent box
In the silence of the white box
In the constant silence
In the constant white
In the white of the white box

Your head starts exploding
Your skull is about to split
Your spine is drilling into your brain
You are pissing your brains away

In the white of the silent box
In the silence of the white box
In the constant silence
In the constant white
In the white of the white box

Under the Nazis an experiment was made in which they locked a man in a white cell with white furniture. He wore white clothes. And all his food and drink were white. He very soon lost his appetite. He could not eat. He could not drink. The sight of the white food and the white drink made him vomit.

Astrid came to England and began life again as Anna. She worked with young people in the East End as an instructor in car mechanics. One Englishwoman says: "Anna gave me and my children enormous support. . . . When I was drinking too much, it was Anna who cared enough to see why and then helped me to make decisions that I was drinking to forget."

This is the Terror Girl of the *Daily Mail*.

Now Anna is being kept under maximum-security conditions in a man's prison — Brixton. There are only two women in the prison. They are supervised by seven warders. They have no privacy. When Anna has a visitor, her conversation is listened to. When her lawyer visits her in her cell below the court, there is always a policeman in the cell. For three hours a day she is allowed to meet the other woman in Brixton jail. The rest of the time she spends on her own.

> So will Anna be sent back by our rulers
> to the white of the white box
> to the silence of the white silence
> to the constant silence and the constant white
> to the whiteness of the silence
> to the silence of the whiteness
> to the whiteness of the whiteness
> to the silence of the silence
> to the whiteness of the whiteness
> to the silence of the silence
> to the whiteness to the silence to the whiteness to
>   the silence
> whiteness   whiteness   silence   silence

Stop. You can stop them. If Anna is extradited or not depends on the Home Secretary. Write to the Home Secretary. Demand she be allowed to stay. Demand that she be treated humanely. And if you are German, force your government to be satisfied with its revenge, to drop its demands for extradition, to drop the case against her, to close the Silent Wing forever.

> We will walk out from here
> into the blue-eyed, brown-faced, green-haired
>   world
> our spinning, singing planet

but Anna who was Astrid lies chained in the box
    of the state
silent men in suits walk towards her with blank
    faces
they carry syringes and hooks and guns in their
    white briefcases

LET ANNA STAY HERE

LET HER WORK

LET HER REST

LET HER FIND LOVE

Screws and Saints

What's worse than the uniformed devils
When they trap you in a concrete hell?
The claws and boots of the angels
When you're savaged in a golden cell.

Nearly Nothing Blues

Well it's six o'clock and I done nearly nothing all day
Yes 6 p.m. — done nearly nothing all day
I'll do half as much tomorrow if I get my way

Four Sorry Lines

Sixteen years old, and you would sneer
At a baby or a phoenix.
Mock on, mock on, in your blue-lidded splendour —
Most well-paid jobs are reserved for cynics.

Action And Reaction Blues

Further back you pull a bow-string
        the further the arrow goes whooshin
Further back Maggie drags us
        the further the revolution

"Appendix IV

Requirements In The Shelter

   Clothing
   Cooking Equipment
   Food
   Furniture
   Hygiene
   Lighting
   Medical
   Shrouds"

What?

   "Shrouds.
   Several large, strong black plastic bags
   and a reel of 2-inch, or wider, adhesive tape
   can make adequate air-tight containers
   for deceased persons
   until the situation permits burial."

No I will not put my lovely wife into a large strong
   black plastic bag
No I will not put my lovely children into large strong
   black plastic bags
No I will not put my lovely dog or my lovely cats into
   large strong black plastic bags

I will embrace them all until I am filled with their
   radiation

43

Then I will carry them, one by one,
Through the black landscape
And lay them gently at the concrete door
Of the concrete block
Where the colonels
And the chief detectives
And the MPs
And the Regional Commissioners
Are biding their time

And then I will lie down with my wife and children
And my dog and my cats

And we will wait for the door to open

My Shy Di In Newspaperland

(All the lines are quoted from the British Press on Royal Engagement day, the only slight distortions appear in the repeats of the four-line chorus. Written in collaboration with Alistair Mitchell.)

Who will sit where in the forest of tiaras?
She is an English rose without a thorn.
Love is in their stars, says Susie.
She has been plunged headfirst into a vast goldfish
    bowl.

Did she ponder as she strolled for an hour through
    Belgravia?
Will they, won't they? Why, yes they will.
They said so yesterday.
He said: "Will you?"
She said: "Yes."
So did his mother — and so say all of us.

Who will sit where in the head of the goldfish?
She is an English forest without a tiara.
Love is in their roses, says Thorny.
She has been plunged starsfirst into a vast susie bowl.

Most of the stories in this issue were written
By James Whitaker, the *Daily Star* man
Who has always known that Diana and Prince Charles
    would marry.
He watched them fishing on the River Dee —
And Lady Diana was watching him too.
She was standing behind a tree using a mirror
To watch James Whitaker at his post,
James Whitaker, the man who always knew.

Who will sit where in the stars of Susie?
She is an English head without a goldfish.
Love is in their forests, says Tiara.
She has been plunged rosefirst into a vast thorn bowl.

All about Di.
Shy Di smiled and blushed.
Lady Di has her eyelashes dyed.
My shy Di.

She descends five times from Charles II —
Four times on the wrong side of the blanket
And once on the right side.

Who will sit where in the rose of thorns?
She is an English star without a susie.
Love is in their heads, says Goldfish.
She has been plunged forestfirst into a vast tiara bowl.

Flatmate Carolyn Pride was in the loo
When she heard of the engagement.
"Lady Diana told me through the door," she said last
    night.
"I just burst into tears. There were floods and floods of
    tears."

Who will sit where in the forest of tiaras?
She is an English rose without a thorn.
Love is in their stars, says Susie.
She has been plunged headfirst into a vast goldfish
    bowl.

Autumnobile

The forest's throat is sore.
Frost-work. Echoing shouts of friends.
October, in her gold-embroidered nightie,
Floating downstream, little mad flowers shimmering.

The silky fur of her
And her hot fingers curling,
Uncurling round and a sudden shove —
There goes my heart tobogganing,

Down snow, slush, ending stuck in the mud,
That's love! O dig me out of here
And glide me off down Pleasure Street
To the sparkle rink where bears go skating.

I ate pancakes at the funeral.
I ate pancakes and ice-cream too.
The mourners drank like musty flies,
All round Summer's coffin, sucking and buzzing.

The days of dust and nights of gnats
Are over and, covered with raindrop warts,
My friend, the most unpopular Season in school,
Smoking and spitting — Autumn's coming.

How do I love that fool, the Fall?
Like Paraquatted nettles. Like
A two-headed 50p. Like a sick shark.
Like a punchy boxer who can't stop grinning.

Sunshine's rationed. Get in the queue
For a yard of colour, a pound of warm.
Deathbed scenes on the video-sky,
Sunsets like Olivier acting dying.

I feel weightless as a child who's built
Out of nursery bricks with ducks and clocks on.
I eat more sleep. I slap more feet.
Autumn — my marzipan flesh is seething.

I open a book and splash straight into it.
The fire reads all my old newspapers.
I freak across the galaxy on Pegasus
And see the cracked old world, rocking and bleeding.

The saloon doors in my skull swing open,
Out stride a posse of cowboy children
Bearing a cauldron of the magic beans
Which always set my poems quivering.

Now my electric typer purrs,
And now it clackers under my fingers'
Flickering. And now the oily engine
Throbs into hubbub. The Autumnobile is leaving.

Nobody on earth knows where on earth they're going
. . . .

(a hell of a long way after Pushkin and Derzhavin)

To My Friends, On My Fiftieth Birthday

My darlings, my friends, makers of all kinds, what can
  I say to them?
Go on with your labours of love, for you build
  Jerusalem.
My friends, my darlings, what can I say about you?
I will love you forever, I would have died without you.

Sally Go Round the Ombelibus On A Thursday Afternoon

(for Sally Stephens)

First time I saw Sally
She was moving through the meadow
Lazing on her mother's lovely arm.

Together in the big marquee
She was just the right size for beauty
Held against my heart,
And I saw her daddy smile
A wider smile.

Milk was warm
Blue air was chilly
Trees and hedges
Danced circles round Sally

Green afternoon
Green afternoon
And my heart filled up again

For Gordon Snell — My Best, First And Finest Friend — On His Fiftieth Birthday

"By and by they all are dead" — stage direction at the end of an early play by Gordon Snell, writer for grown-ups and children.
"By and by is easily said" — Hamlet in *Hamlet*, a part once played by Gordon Snell.

By and by they all are dead —
The people, animals, earth and sky.
By and by is easily said.

Any child who has ever read
Knows that Book People cannot die.
By and by they all are dead?

Peter Rabbit's still raiding the potting shed
Under Long John Silver's laser eye.
By and by is easily said,

But Alice and the Golux tread
Emerald Oz where the Jumblies fly.
By and by they all are dead?

Lorna Doone and Just William wed
Where The Wild Things Are with Harriet the Spy.
By and by is easily said. . . .

Gordon — the creatures your fancy has bred
Shall live with them — that's the sweet By-and-
    By!
By and by they all are dead?
By and by is easily said!

Shoot-out At The Hebden Bridge Saloon

(for Joy Smedley)

Pony Express rider
leaned down and muttered:
Watch out for the Gold-Dust Kid,
gonna be the fastest. . . .
then he hit the horizon with his horse.

Waited awhile. . .
I'm takin a taste at the bar
when this gold-colour kid
kinda jumpy
but Apache eyes
moseys in, tosses a bag of dust on the bar —
Bourbon.

You the Gold-Dust Kid?

Yup.

Heard you're fast.

Yup.

Show me.

We locked eyes.
Made my move.

In through my ribs
out through my backbone.

Pour a last whiskey down me, Doc
And — watch out for the Gold-Dust Kid,
She. . . .

52

For Nigel And Delyth

Mumbles, June 1982

Nightfall: the harp is playing like a fountain.
The harp is dancing like a happy woman.
The heartbeat of the house is the harp
As it sings like the spinning world.

Young Merlin splashes in the generous fountain.
He eats and drinks happiness with his woman
And the sea lies below them like a mighty harp
And his making table is a brown field in a new world.

To Elizabeth Quinn on the First Night Of "Children Of A Lesser God" In London

25 August 1981

Tonight I saw a thousand birds
   Nobody knew their names
A thousand birds in flight
   a thousand birds
Tonight I saw a thousand birds

For the Eightieth Birthday of Hoagy Carmichael

22 November 1979

Hoagland — white waterfall piano keys!
Old rockin' chairs to help us all think mellow!
Always-Fall forests of star-tall trees
Growing chords of gold, brown, red and yellow!
Yes, Hoagland, friendliest of all countries.

Casual is, I guess, as casual does,
And you casually sing and casually knock us sideways.
Rolling songs riding the river's tideways,
Mist-songs gliding, city-songs that buzz.
I wander Hoagland pathways when dusk falls.
Celia strolls with me as wild and tame
Hoagland bird-folk enchant us with their calls.
Anyone who has ears grins at your name.
Eighty years of great songs! I wish you would
Live on as long as your good Hoagland life feels good.

Notes:
a. Hoagland is Mr Carmichael's official Christian name
b. Celia is my wife's name.

Sardinia, 1979

(for Boty)

Yellow   lampshine   through   the   leaves   of   the
    tambourine.
Black waves of jelly slapping the white jetty.
Forty grandfathers sit round a Victorian tree.
Five of us are discussing our spaghetti.

To Michael Bell

(my teacher at Greenways School whose motto was: "A Green Thought In A Green Shade.")

In the second year of the Slaughter
I attended a school in Hell
Feeling like King Lear's fourth daughter
Strapped down in a torture cell
Then my blue and white mother appeared to me
And she saw I was all afraid
So I was transported mysteriously
To a green school in a green shade

And there I met a great mechanic
And he mended my twisted wings
And he gentled away my panic
And he showed me how a vision sings
And I thank Michael Bell most lovingly
For the mountains and lakes he made
And the way he shone the light of peace on me
Like a green thought in a green shade

Loony Prunes

(an apology poem for my daughter)

We played the savage ludo which is known as Coppit,
Chatted, drank wine, ate lamb, played Beatle tunes
And then we started it, found we couldn't stop it —
A contest to eat maximum loony prunes.

They weren't just the ordinary, wrinkled, black,
Laxative fruit imported from — who knows?
But, floating in a stinging pool of Armagnac,
They were sozzled Français lunatic pruneaux.

Then, indoor fireworks, and the sharp flashes
Of three-second sparklers, dull horse-races,
A wonderful serpent, a frilly fern of ashes —
While the loony prune-juice flushed our faces.

As I was trying to put the fireworks out
We started arguing like sun and moon.
I grabbed you as the whole world seemed to shout.
You ran upstairs. I'm sorry. I'm a loony prune.

Falling Feathers

(for Andy and Gill on their wedding day
Saturday, 7 May 1983)

watch out for falling feathers
golden sailboats in the air
watch out for falling feathers
or they'll settle in your hair

      and you'll look pretty silly with golden feathers
      thrilling all over your nut
      you'll never get a mentionable pensionable job
      you'll live in a hut with a wooden water-butt

      you'll have to sidle round the countryside side-
         ways
      dancing to the music of bats
      attempting to make a magical living
      cutting rabbits in half producing girls out of hats

o watch out for falling feathers
golden rockinghorses in the air
watch out for falling feathers
or they'll settle in your hair

      and you'll be no better than your singing
      and no better than your audience too
      and you'll be no better than feathers falling
      golden golden down the blue

      and you'll be no better than hedgehogs
      who can only live like hedgehogs live
      and you'll be no better than the holy Jumblies
      who went to sea like you in a sieve

yes watch out for falling feathers
golden lions prowling down the air
watch out for falling feathers
or they'll settle in your hair

      ten miles overhead there's a couple of angels
      loving in a cloud on springs
      and they got a little archangelic
      and a couple of feathers jumped off of their wings

      so live like a couple of featherheads
      who got married on Uppendown Hill
      for the feathers fell off a pair of angels
      whose names coincidentally are Andy and Jill

watch out for falling feathers
golden cradles in the air
watch out for falling feathers
and catch them and save them
and take them and place them
golden in your children's hair

watch out for falling feathers
golden in the golden air
watch out for falling feathers
and they'll settle in your hair
in your happyeverafter hair

Bring Out Your Nonsense

A detective-sergeant walks into the police station
A woman with a floor at home inspects the carpet
  store
A train stops at the platform after deceleration
Librarians enter the library through the library door
Telephonists at the switchboard are answering
  telephones
A Telegraph reader buys the Telegraph from the paper
  shop
Cars drive, pedestrians walk and my heart groans
As out of the Billericay copshop steps a cop

But I'm wrong — the cop debags himself to give birth
  to a phoenix
Which zips down the High Street with Dizzy Gillespian
  squeals
And the silver and gold melts in all the jewellers'
  windows
And the town is crotch-deep in whirlpools of syrup
And you sail over the horizon in a pea-blue schooner
Bearing the wild good news you sail bearing the good
  wild food
Over the horizon with a ton of friends playing magical
  banjoes
And the people of Billericay dance in delirious dozens

First Poem Composed In A Dream

A snub-nosed woman holding a jug;
Maybe it will be empty
By 1969 or nineteen-sempty. . . .

Second Poem Composed In A Dream

"Let's get married!"

"But I can't remember my name."

"Let's get suffocated then!"

Daydream Number 157,423

In a quiet afternoon drinking club
In a leather-upholstered booth
I wish I was listening to Billie Holiday
Telling the poisonous truth

24 Orders With (Optional) Adjectives

fetch my (happy) screwdriver
smell those (sugary) goldfish
shut that (amazing) door
touch my (scrawny) statues
close your (intricate) eyes
fill up the (Russian) hole again
tell your (gaping) sister
put that (shining) bomb together
spare my (murky) child
show your (grey) feelings
put up your (smiling) hand
hide your (iron) face
hand over those (solemn) emeralds
don't try to get (red-handled) funny with me
wash their (impertinent) car
cut its (sweet) throat
eat your (exclusive) cabbage
take down your (little) trousers
make up your (agile) mind
get down on your (frightening) knees
stick to your own (pathetic) kind
take the (stupid) tea
polish those (harmonious) boots

Reassuring Song If Your Name Is Mitchell

A million Mitchells sing this song
A million Mitchells can't be wrong
We are a million Mitchells strong
Why don't you just sing along?
Why don't you just sing along?
    Happy-go-zombie,
    Hello Abercrombie!
With a million marching Mitchells

Chile In Chains

"Student demonstrators yesterday forced the Chilean Ambassador to clamber over roof-tops and hide in a kitchen after they broke up a meeting he was trying to address at St John's College, Cambridge.

"The Ambassador, Professor Miguel Schweitzer, was invited to talk to the Monday Club on diplomatic relations between Britain and Chile ..." *The Guardian*, 13 November 1980.

"Any victory for the people, however small, is worth celebrating" — a demonstrator.

"I've never seen an Ambassador running before, so I'm not quite sure how to rate him as a runner" — a Cambridge spectator.

There's eight men in Cambridge called the Monday
    Club,
It's like the British Movement with brains,
And they thought it cute to pay a sort of tribute
To the government of Chile in Chains.

So the Mondays invited the Ambassador
To St John's as their honoured guest —
But he must come unto them secretly
(At the Special Branch's special request).

The Ambassador was glad to get an invite —
He flicked off his electric shock machine,
Scrubbed the blood from under his fingernails
And summoned his bodyguard and limousine.

"What shall I tell them?" the Ambassador mused
As he flushed his better self down the loo,
"Allende was a mass murderer
But Pinochet is Jesus Mark Two?

66

"What shall I tell them?" the Ambassador thought
As his car snaked down Cambridgeshire lanes,
"That Victor Jara tortured himself to death
And Paradise is Chile in Chains?"

But as they were proffering South African sherry
The faces of the Monday Club froze —
For a mob of Lefties had assembled outside:
Socialist and Anarchist desperadoes!

So they switched their venue from the Wordsworth
    Room
To the Wilberforce Room, locked the doors
And the Monday Club gave its limp applause
To a pimp for fascist whores.

But the revolution never stops
(We even go marching when it rains),
And a Yale lock is no protection at all
For a salesman for Chile in Chains.

When the Left tumbled into the Wilberforce Room
The Ambassador was terrified.
His bodyguard shovelled him out the back door
And the Monday Club was occupied.

Oh they hurried him over the rooftops
And the pigeons gave him all they had.
Oh they hid him away in the kitchen
And all of the food went bad.

But the Left sat down in the Wilberforce Room.
The atmosphere smelled of shame.
Then a Don said: "This is private property.
Tell me your college and name."

"We didn't come to talk about property.
We came to talk about the pains

Of the poor and the murdered and the tortured and the
    raped
Who are helpless in Chile in Chains."

They grouped a scrum of cops round their honoured
    guest
And we jeered at him and his hosts
As he ran with the cops across the grass of the Court
Like a torturer pursued by ghosts.

He galloped with his minders to his limousine
But the stink of his terror remains
And everyone who watched his cowardly run
Knows — Chile will tear off her chains.

A Prayer For The Rulers Of This World

God bless their suits
God bless their ties
God bless their grubby
Little alibis

God bless their firm,
Commanding jaws
God bless their thumbs
God bless their claws

God bless their livers
God bless their lungs
God bless their
Shit-encrusted tongues

God bless their prisons
God bless their guns
God bless their deaf and dumb
Daughters and sons

God bless their corpuscles
God bless their sperms
God bless their souls
Like little white worms

Oh God will bless
The whole bloody crew
For God, we know,
Is a ruler too

And the blessed shall live
And the damned shall die
And God will rule
In his suit and his tie

Ode To George Melly

If Bonzo the Dog got resurrected he could leap like you
If Satan the Snake ate Adam's birthday cake he would
    creep like you
If Liz Bat Queen wasn't pound-note green she'd hand
    the Crown to you —
For nothing on earth falls down like George Melly do.

About Suffering They Were Never Wrong
The Old Mistresses

Bessie Smith
And Big Joe Turner
Make Othello
Sound like a learner

All Darks Are Alike In The Death

As you crouch on my chest
I'll stroke your fur
Funny old death
Purr   purr   purr   purr

Smilers

When Woody Allen smiles
From the attics of the town
The secretary tears
Come rolling down

When John Wayne smiles
Boy you better grin
Or he'll be obliged
To kick your feelings in

Buy A Sprig Of Haggis For Bad Luck, Sir?

Have you ever been pregnant on Euston Station?
And they said you'd be met at your destination
By a fixer who'd be wearing an Asian carnation
And you stare around the concourse in consternation
For it's the annual outing of the Royal Association
For the Propagation of the Asian Carnation.
Have you ever been pregnant on Euston Station?

A Sunset Cloud Procession Passing Ralph Steadman's House

1. A cigar-smoking porker drags a small hay-cart from which a jewelled crocodile smiles and waves.

2. A black fried egg struts by, one woolly eyebrow raised like Noel Coward.

3. An emaciated caribou clanks along.

4. An ant-eater inflates a smoker's-lung balloon.

5. Eskimo Jim pulls Auntie Hippo tail-first, but she hangs on to her perambulator full of hippolets.

6. They are pursued by a neolithic Hoover.

7. And followed by Leonardo's Tin Lizzie and Michelangelo as a tumescent frogman, pride of the Sexual Boat Service.

8. A simple mushroom shape, rising one inch every four seconds.

9. Father Time with a crumpled scythe.

10. A whale spouting black shampoo all over its own humpy head.

11. A cocker spaniel taking a free ride on the backbone of a boa-constrictor.

12. And up from out of the dark hill's shoulders rise the shoulders of another, larger, darker hill.

Dinner With The Dons of Saint Abysmas's College, Oxbridge

I am the spy from Ignorance,
In my thundercloud gown I dine.
I am the Elephant Man who sits
Between Will Hay and Wittgenstein.

Bury My Bones With An Eddy Merckx

live people don't often
have eyes for the overhead stars
but gloom down roads
in micro-wave cars

they dunno how the rippling
of the wild air feels
frowning round town
in tombs on wheels

but ghosts ride bikes
free-wheeling mostly
singing songs like
Give It To Me Ghostly

ghosts got no rooty-tooty
duty to be done
cars are for bloody business
bikes for fun

Give It To Me Ghostly

give it to me ghostly
close-up and long-distance
i've an open policy
of misty non-resistance

so give it to me ghostly
shudder up and lisp a
bogey-woman promise
to your will o' the whisper

give it to me ghostly
spook it to me somehow
haunt me haunt me haunt me
oooo thanks i've come now

Who Goes Where?

Oh who is that man who wishes he'd stuck to the path
His suede shoes uncomfortably soaked in the dews of
   the lawn?
Oh that is the man with the face of a sad sardine,
     And they call him Overdrawn.

Activities Of An East And West Dissident Blues

(Verses to be read by the Secret Police, the chorus to be read by anyone else.)

When I woke up this morning it was nothing
o'clock
I erased all the dreams from my head
I washed my face in shadow-juice
And for breakfast I ate my bed

I said goodbye to my jailer and spy
Burnt letters from all of my friends
Then I caught the armoured bus for a mystery
tour
To the street with two dead ends

and oh
I wish I had a great big shiny brass diver's helmet
and I wish I had great big leaden diver's boots on me
and I wish I had infallible mates upstairs at the
air-pumps
as I wandered forever on the bottom of the great free
sea

I arrived at my factory or office or field
I did what I was meant to do
I left undone what should be left undone
And all of the others did the same thing too
And you too? Right.

In the evening I read whatever should be read
Listened to whatever should be heard
And I taught the top twenty government slogans
To my golden-caged security bird

And I changed into the pair of pyjamas
With a number stamped on brown and black bars
And I pulled down the blind to keep out of my
    mind
The excitement of the stars

but oh
I wish I had a great big shining brass diver's helmet
and I wish I had great big leaden diver's boots on me
and infallible mates upstairs with their hands on the
    air-pumps
as I wandered forever on the bottom of the great green
    flowing free and easy sea

New Skipping Rhymes

Good little Georgie
Worked like a madman
Three years at Oxford
Five years an Adman
Went on Mastermind
Did so well on that show
Now he's the Host
Of a TV Chat Show

My savings are my baby
Money is my boss
My mummy and my daddy
Were profit and loss
One thousand, two thousand, three thousand, four. . . .

Meat on the hook
Powder in the jar
Mickey Jagger is a Star
S-T-A-R spells Star
He can whistle
He can hum
He can wriggle his umpumbum

Pretty little Pam
Passed her exam
What shall we give her?
Doughnuts with jam

Stupid little Sam
Failed his exam
What shall we give him?
Who gives a damn?

The High School Bikeshed

Yellow stairs
Do the zig-zag stagger.
In the red shed
The bikes are snogging.
Silver, they whisper to each other,
Silver, silver.

Staying Awake

Monday came so I fucked off to school
School is a big huge building
Where you're not supposed to get any fucking sleep
We hung around till they counted us in a room
With pictures of fucking owls and bats
Then we hung around some more

Miss Harburton ponced in and yelled about
How her fucking bike's gone missing who cares
Then we all fucked off to another room

It was Mister Collins from Outer Space
Talked about not leaving gum stuck around
And Queen Victoria up the Suez Canal
And how he wouldn't let us act out
The Death of General Gordon again
Not ever and no he never saw Chainsaw Massacre
And no didn't want to even free
On Goodgeman's sexy mother's video
And Beano Black said his mother was poorly
And started to give us the fucking grisly details
Saved by the bell and we hung around
Smoking in the bog and not getting any sleep

Then we all fucked off to another room
And it was Mrs Grimes Environmental Studies
So I finally got my fucking sleep.

I stay out of trouble but in my head
I'm bad I'm fucking bad as they come
When I die they'll punish me
For the things I done in my fucking head.

They'll send me off to a big huge building
And they won't let me get any fucking sleep.
Well that's what I reckon
Death is like fucking off
To another fucking school.

The Reindeer Rider In An Old Russian Photograph

The reindeer rider could only speak
A Russian brand of Turkish
While the best that I can manage
Is a sort of British English.
Besides the reindeer rider died
In the last century
While I'm in the top front left-hand seat
Of a double-decker called Mortuary.
But seeing him on that reindeer's back
I want to warn him to pin his ears back,
For, while he seems to think: so far so good,
That reindeer is obviously a no-good
And its eye is full of mischief
As an oak is full of oak-wood.

Carol During The Falklands Experience

In the blind midslaughter
The drowned sank alone
Junta set like concrete
Thatcher like a stone

Blood had fallen, blood on blood,
Blood on blood
In the blind midslaughter
In the madness flood

What shall I give them
Powerless as I am?
If I were a rich man
I wouldn't give a damn

If I were an arms dealer
I would play my part —
All I can do is point towards
The holy human heart.

Third Opinion

"Is he better off with it or without it?"
Said the doctor with the moustache.
Said the doctor with the beard:
"Well, frankly, Simon, I'm in two minds about it."
They turned to the bed.
The patient had disappeared.

Money And Booze

(a love song)

He was as filthy as fivepence
And vacant as ginger-beer shandy
But she was as naughty as ninepence
And she went through his system like brandy

Social Being

"Come to the party! Isn't it time
You faced the world again?"
So I clenched my face and entered the place —
A roomful of boozing Mister Men.

Remember Red Lion Square?

I haven't heard any Moderates lately
Mention the name of Kevin Gateley,
The student who, so the Coroner said,
Died from "a moderate blow to the head".

The Christians Are Coming Goodbye Goodbye

They fought the good fight on six continents,
Cutting down the godless foe.
The Christians were Super-Campbells,
The whole world — their Glencoe.

Ode To Her

You so draggy Ms Maggie
The way you drag us down
The way you shake your finger
Way you frown your frown
But a day's soon dawning
When all the world will shout
We're gonna catch yer Ms Thatcher
You'll be dragged out

You so draggy Ms Maggie
You tore this land apart
With your smile like a laser
And your iceberg heart
You teach the old and jobless
What poverty means
You send the young men killing
The Irish and the Argentines

You so draggy Ms Maggie
With your million cuts
You slashed this country
Till it spilled its guts
You crucified parents
And their children too
Nailed em up by the million
Here's what we'll do

You so draggy Ms Maggie
Madonna of the Rich
We're gonna introduce you
On the Anfield pitch
Oh you can talk your meanest
But you as good as dead
When Yosser Hughes butts you
With his poor old head. . . .

How To Be Extremely Saintly, Rarefied And Moonly

(For Becky, who, when I spoke about resisting my urge to lie around watching videotapes all day told me: "Let your temptation never fail you.")

Let your coconut be your guide
Let the sun stew in its own juice
Let your coat and rent your hat
And let your temptation never fail you

Let the good times roller-skate
Let me inside-out please, I forgot my keys
Let the flim-flam floogie with the floy-floy rock 'n' roll
But let your temptation never fail you

Let the lecturer be harangued by the blackboard
Let your letters stamp their footling feet to better letter
    music
Let us play soccer together with a bonny lettuce
And in the Beantime —
Let your temptation, Becky, never fail you.

Land Of Dopes And Loonies

William Shakespeare was loony
Burns was a maniac too
Milton was thoroughly crackers
Yeats was a looney all through
Edward Lear, Shelley and Coleridge,
Whitman and Lawrence and Blake
What a procession of nutters
Looning for poetry's sake
All of the poets were dafties
Dafter when the going got rough
All except William Wordsworth
Who wasn't nearly crazy enough

Leonardo was loopy
So was Toulouse Lautrec
Bosch had all of his screws loose
Van Gogh's head was a wreck
Pablo Picasso was batty
Just take a look at his work
Rembrandt was out of his windmill
Brueghel was bloody berserk
All of the painters were bonkers
In the barmy army of art
All except Sir Joshua Reynolds
And he was a wealthy old Humpty Dumpty. . . .

On The Beach At Cambridge

I am assistant to the Regional Commissioner
At Block E, Brooklands Avenue,
Communications Centre for Region 4,
Which used to be East Anglia.

I published several poems as a young man
But later found I could not meet my own high
    standards
So tore up all my poems and stopped writing.
(I stopped painting at eight and singing at five.)
I was seconded to Block E
From the Ministry for the Environment.

Since there are no established poets available
I have come out here in my MPC
(Maximum Protective Clothing),
To dictate some sort of poem or word-picture
Into a miniature cassette recorder.

When I first stepped out of Block E on to this beach
I could not record any words at all,
So I chewed two of the orange-flavoured pills
They give us for morale, switched on my Sony
And recorded this:

I am standing on the beach at Cambridge.
I can see a group in their MPC
Pushing Hoover-like and Ewbank-like machines
Through masses of black ashes.
The taller men are soldiers or police,
The others, scientific supervisors.
This group moves slowly across what seems
Like an endless car park with no cars at all.

I think that, in one moment,
All the books in Cambridge
Leapt off their shelves,
Spread their wings
And became white flames
And then black ash.
And I am standing on the beach at Cambridge.

You're a poet, said the Regional Commissioner,
Go out and describe that lot.

The University Library — a little hill of brick-dust.
King's College Chapel — a dune of stone-dust.
The sea is coming closer and closer.

The clouds are edged with green,
Sagging low under some terrible weight.
They move more rapidly than usual.

Some younger women with important jobs
Were admitted to Block E
But my wife was a teacher in her forties.
We talked it over
When the nature of the crisis became apparent.
We agreed somebody had to carry on.
That day I kissed her goodbye as I did every day
At the door of our house in Chesterton Road.
I kissed my son and my daughter goodbye.
I drove to Block E beside Hobson's Brook.
I felt like a piece of paper
Being torn in half.

And I am standing on the beach at Cambridge.
Some of the men in their MPC
Are sitting on the ground in the black ashes.
One is holding his head in both his hands.

I was forty-two three weeks ago.
My children painted me
Bright-coloured cards with poems for my birthday.
I stuck them with Blue-tack on the kitchen door.
I can remember the colours.

But in one moment all the children in Cambridge
Spread their wings
And became white flames
And then black ash.

And the children of America, I suppose.
And the children of Russia, I suppose.

And I am standing on the beach at Cambridge
And I am watching the broad black ocean tide
Bearing on its shoulders its burden of black ashes.

And I am listening to the last words of the sea
As it beats its head against the dying land.

Cambridge, March 1981

96